Adult Coloring Book

Healing Flowers

Stress Relieving Patterns

E.S. Carruthers

ISBN-13: 978-1530587209
ISBN-10: 1530587204

Color to relieve stress! This is my calming coloring book. Each picture will relax and renew you. Every flower was hand drawn with healing energy. You will find 20 complex designs made of simple patterns. Find the hidden meanings and positive affirmations! Coloring is hours of fun and makes a perfect gift.

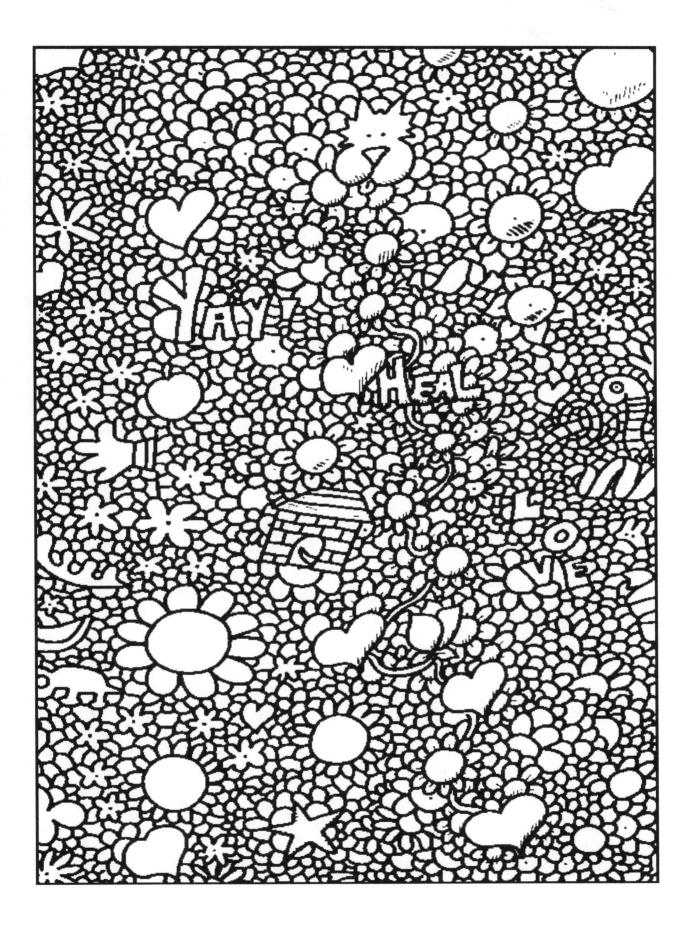

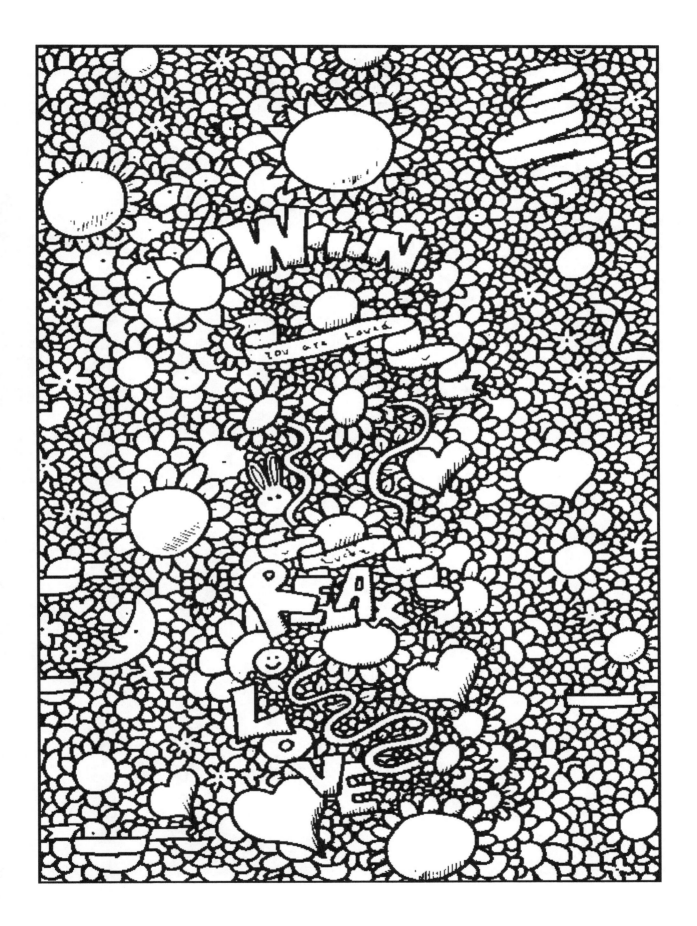

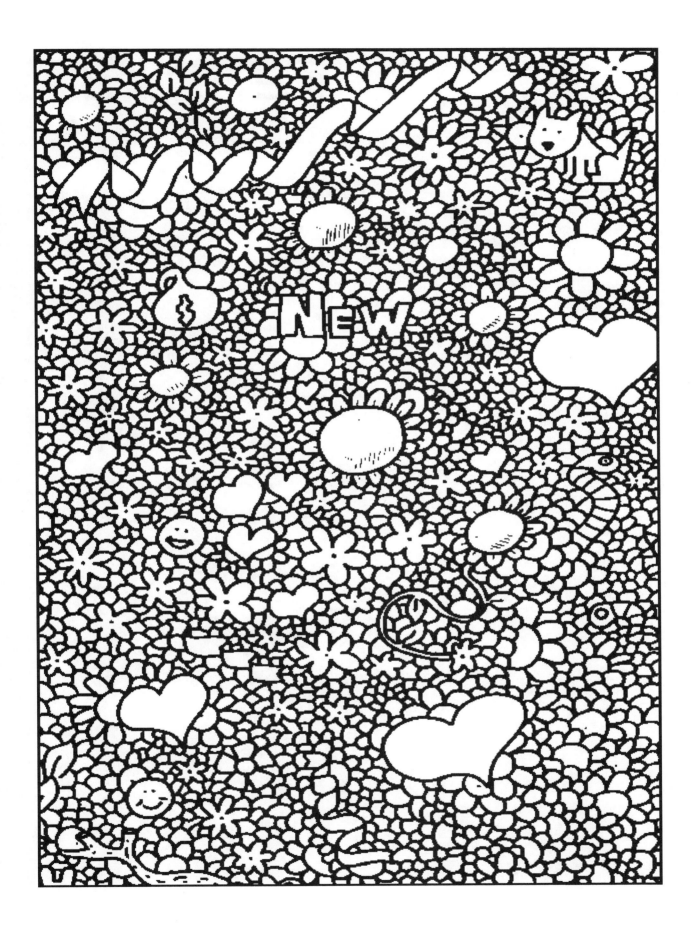

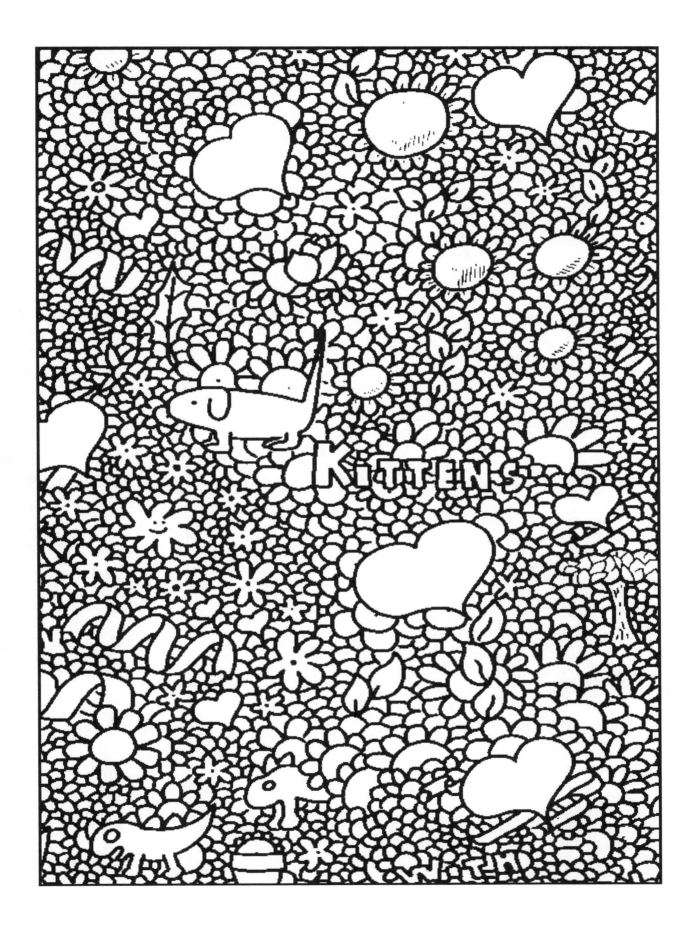

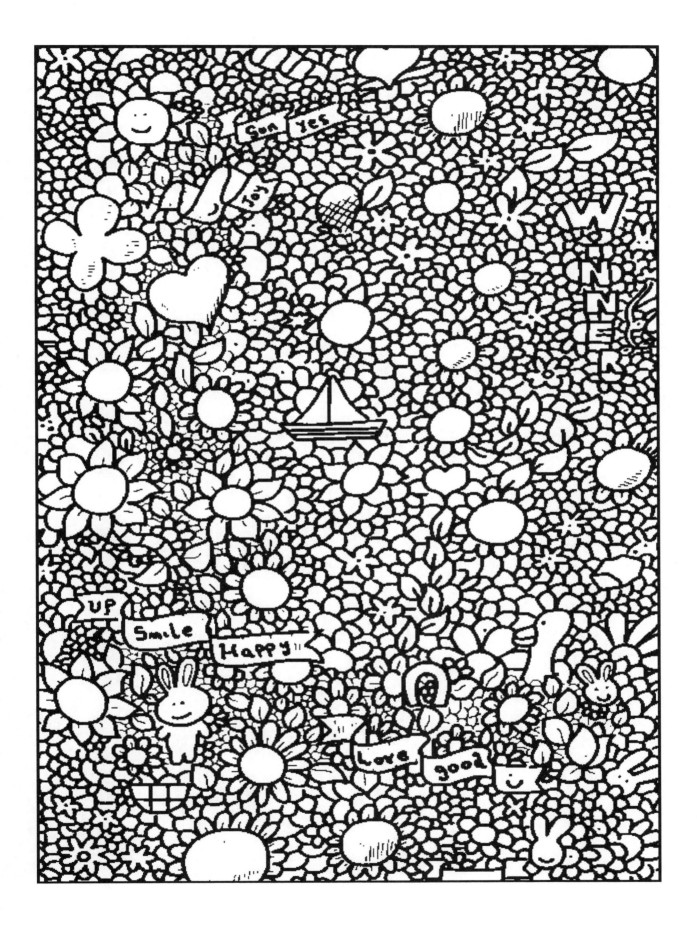

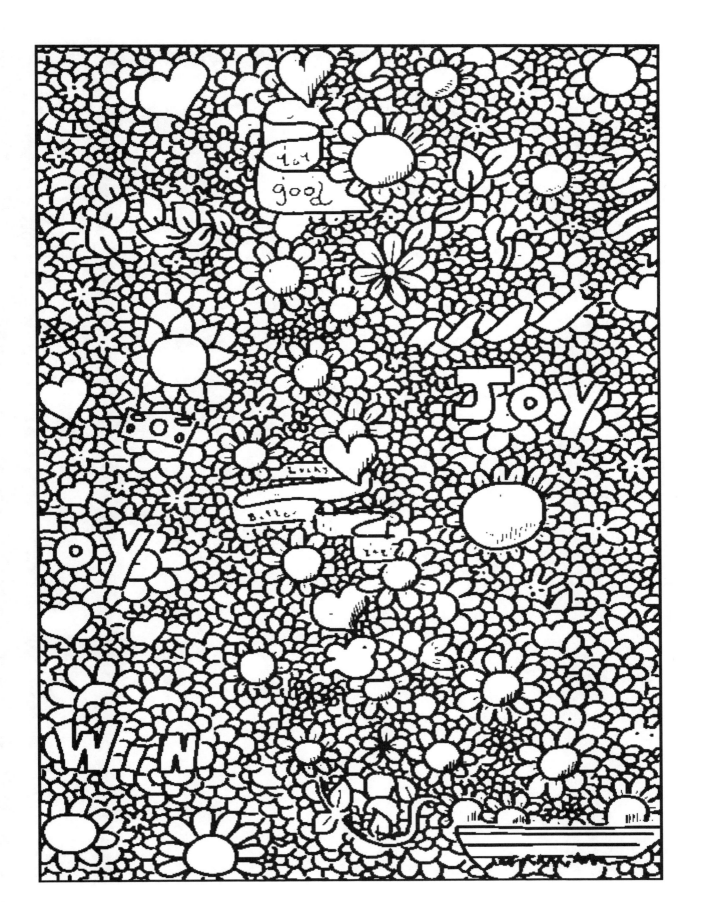

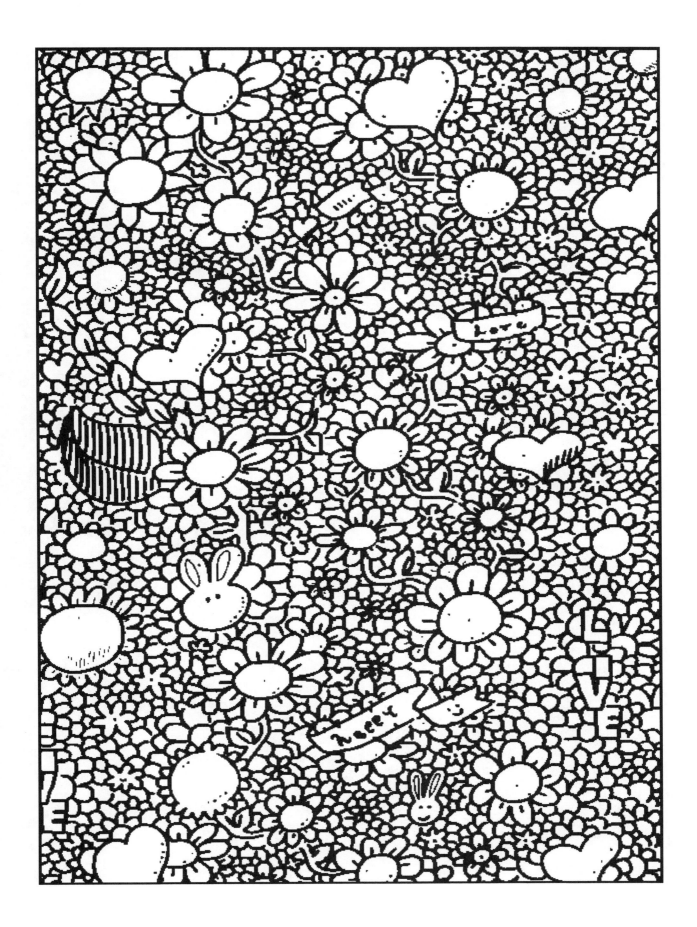

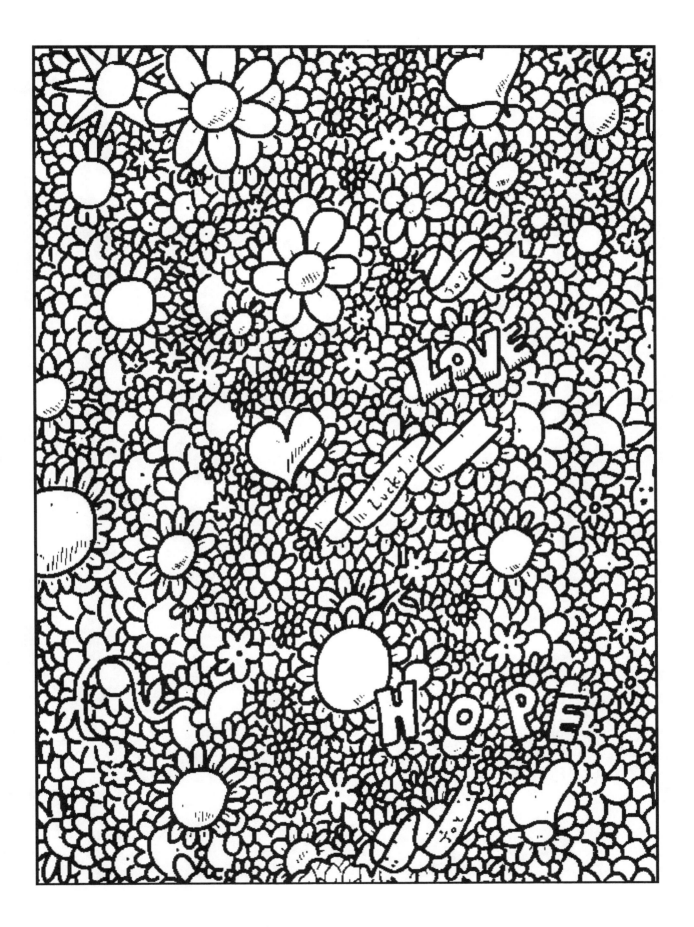

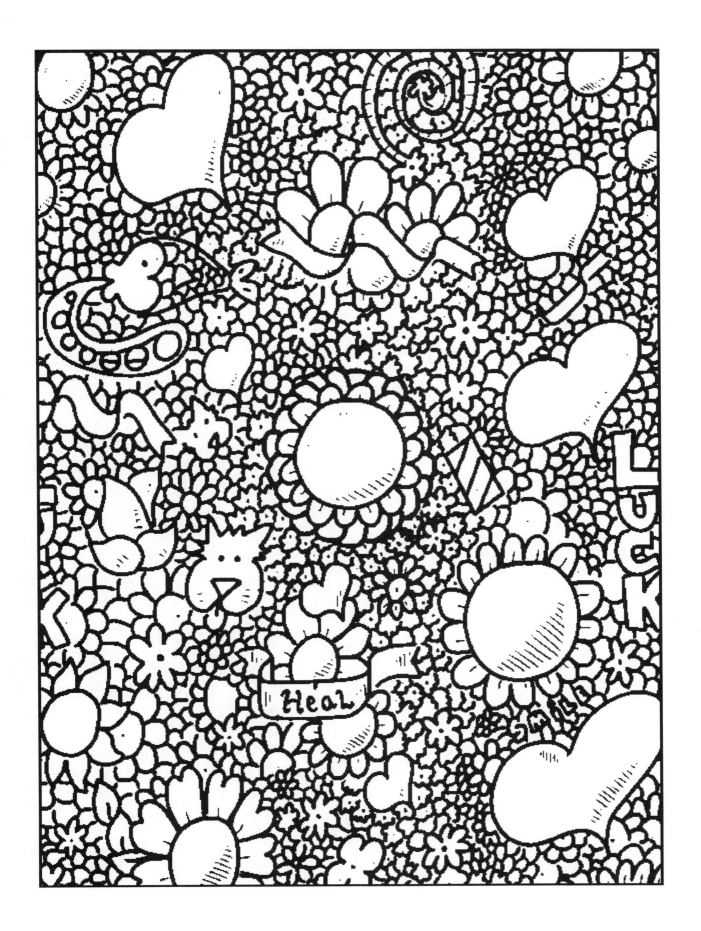

25430126R00024